For more than a century, compositions typified by the selections in this book, had been the delights of both flutists and audiences.

The instrumentalists who specialized in this virtuosity had an enthusiastic and faithful following among the public.

I lived the last years of this happy epoch and often had the pleasure of obtaining large personal success from playing in the second part of a program one of these brillant pieces after satisfying the desires of the promoter in performing a work of a contemporary composer in the first part.

These pieces hardly ever find performance Today.

I am under the impression that most American flutists are ignorant even of the names of theirs composers.

Was it right to abandon these works? Have their places in our repertoire been taken by other compositions of equal value?

I wonder if the flutists of our day are sufficed with the perfunctory acclaim which so often marks the extent of their success.

I should like to know with what the "purists" propose to replace these popular themes — simple, agreeable, evocative — which permitted the composers and flutists to develop the sentiments of expression, the virtuosity and enthusiasm by means of variations demonstrating equally the different qualities of the flute.

After some reflection on this matter I have decided to re-acquaint the young players of our day with the works of this period. The purpose of this book, then, is to present a good, valuable collection of solos for those who love their instrument and have the ability to achieve the advantageous results of mastering these works.

The study of variations develops in many ways the expression, charm and arabesque brillance deployed among various rhythms and rapid passages, all of which renders easy joy to a concert public more responsive (and gratified by) the pleasures of expressive technic than to the clamorous demands of a hopeless metaphysical problem.

Marcel Moyse - (Brattleboro Vt. 17 april 64)

出版にあたって

　1979年に出版以来、世界中の多くの優れたフルーティスト達によって愛用されて来た『ゴールデン・エージ』1. 2. 巻に、完結編として第3巻を加えることにしました。1. 2. 巻出版の時から、モイーズ先生が楽譜のページ数が許すならば、追加したいと考えられていた4つの名曲が残されていたからです。これらの曲はモイーズ先生がレッスンの折り、特に気合いを入れて指導していた、いわくつきの曲ばかりであり、又、後世に是非残したいと望まれていた曲でもあります。

　シャミナードと個人的にも知遇であったモイーズ先生は「セシールはこの部分をこういう風に良く口ずさんでいた」とレッスンの折り、コンチェルティーノについて良く回想されていました。セゲールの〈ガンの思い出〉も特に思い入れの強い曲だったらしく、モイーズ先生の語り草になっている名演が残されています。これは全音版『ヴィルトゥオーソ・フルート名曲集』に付帯のCDで聞くことができます。ドゥメルスマンの〈トレモロ〉はモイーズの師であったエネバンの歴史的名演があります。これらの名演はいずれもSP時代の録音で、時間の制約の為、全曲が収録されている訳ではありませんが、本編では全曲の楽譜を収載してあります。又〈オベロンによる大幻想曲〉はドゥメルスマンの作品の中でも特に傑作とされる曲で、モイーズ先生も『トーンディヴェロップメント』の中で何度も活用していますし、フルーティスト達にとっても、コンサートの折に自分のテクニックや音楽性を十分に発揮できる重要なレパートリーの1つになっています。これらの名曲が、1. 2. 巻同様、優れたフルーティスト達によって大いに演奏され、立派な形で後世に伝えられることを、今は亡きモイーズ先生と共に心より念願するものです。

2000年10月
松本にて　髙橋利夫

改訂にあたって

　モイーズ先生が編集した『ゴールデン・エージ』のオリジナル版には、最終曲にラロのバレエ音楽〈ナムナ〉のフルート・ソロが収められていましたが、ピアノ伴奏譜が無かったため出版できませんでした。この度モイーズ先生がオーケストラの中で吹いているSPから採譜したピアノ伴奏譜が実現し、『ゴールデン・エージ』を名実共に完結できることは、この上ない喜びです。御尽力いただいた作曲家 丸山嘉夫氏に心から感謝を申し上げます。

2008年11月
松本にて　髙橋利夫

THE GOLDEN AGE OF THE FLUTISTS VOL.3

Chosen and revised by Marcel Moyse
Supervised by Toshio Takahashi

演奏会用フルート名曲集

ゴールデン・エージ 3

マルセル・モイーズ──編　髙橋利夫──監修

zen-on music

　1世紀以上にわたって、この本の中に選ばれたような作品は、フルーティストと聴衆の両方にとって欠くことのできないものであった。その道の名手といわれる器楽奏者達は皆自分たちの熱烈で忠実なファンを聴衆の中にもっていた。

　私はこの幸福な時代の晩年に生き、プログラムの前半で現代作品を演奏してファンの要望を満たした後で、後半にこれらの華麗な作品を演奏して、私自身の大きな成功を獲得するという喜びをしばしば味わったものである。

　しかしこれらの作品は現在ではほとんど演奏されることがないし、多分世界のフルーティストのほとんど皆が、この作曲者達の名前すら知らないのではないだろうか。はたしてこれらの作品を捨ててしまって良いものだろうか、我々のレパートリーの中でこれらの作品がしめるべき位置が、これと真に同等の価値があると思われない他の作品と、おきかえられていっているのではないだろうか。演奏の成功の度合いをただ表面的に表しているだけの儀礼的な拍手に、現在のフルーティスト達は満足しているのだろうか。

　私は他の作品でこれらのポピュラーな旋律と真におきかえられるほどの曲があるとしたら、どんな曲か知りたい。これらの旋律は単純で快く、喝采を呼び起こしてくれる。情緒豊かな表現とフルート独特な性格とを共に聞かせてくれる変奏という手段によって、作曲家とフルーティストが名人芸と熱狂とを盛り上げていくことを可能にしてくれる。

　従ってこの本の目的は自分の楽器を愛し、これらの作品を征服できるだけの能力のある人々に、すばらしい価値ある独奏曲をプレゼントすることにある。

　変奏曲の練習は多くの点で表現力と、演奏の魅力を増すのに役立ち、さまざまなリズムと速いパッセージの中で展開されるアラベスクのような華麗さを上達させてくれる。これらすべてがコンサートの聴衆にくつろいだ楽しみを与えてくれるのである。彼らはどうしようもない難解なプログラムを無理やり聞かされるよりも、表情豊かなテクニックの方により反応し満足してくれるに違いないと思う。

マルセル・モイーズ

ヴァーモント州 ブラトルボロにて　1964年4月17日記す

On This Occasion to Publish Volume III

Volume III now joins Volumes I and II, as the concluding volume, of *The Golden Age of the Flutists*, which have been affectionately used by many distinguished flutists in the world ever since their publication in 1979. The underlying circumstance is that four masterpieces were left which Maestro Marcel Moyse wanted to include in the earlier volumes if the available space had permitted. All the four are special ones, which the maestro taught me with particular enthusiasm when he gave me lessons, and which he wanted to hand down to the future generations by all means.

Mr. Moyse, who also was a personal friend of Chaminade, often talked of *Concertino* during his lessons, saying, "Cécile would often hum this part in this way." *Souvernir de Gand* by Seghers seems to have been a piece of particular personal importance to the maestro, who left a distinguished recording of this piece. His performance is still often on the lips of music lovers. The reader can listen to this recording on a CD appended to *Virtuoso Concert Pieces* published by Zen-on Music Company, Ltd. *Le Tremolo* by Demersseman found a historical master performance by Adolphe Hennebains, from whom the maestro learned the flute. These excellent performances were all recorded on 78 rpm discs, which do not necessarily include the whole piece of each because of the limited time capacity of 78 rpm records, but in this volume they are published in their full lengths. *Grande Fantaisie de Concert sur "Obéron"* is acclaimed as a particularly distinguished piece among Demersseman's works. It is used by Mr. Moyse many times in his *Tone Development*, and also constitutes an important part of the repertoires of many flutists as a piece enabling them to fully demonstrate their techniques and musicality. It is my heartfelt wish, and certainly a wish of the late Mr. Moyse, that these masterpieces will be played by flute virtuosi as often as those included in Volumes I and II, and handed down to future generations in a creditable form which they deserve.

October 2000

Toshio Takahashi
In Matsumoto

A Note on the Revision

The original *Golden Age* edited by Mr. Moyse included at the end a flute solo piece from Lalo's ballet music *Namouna*, but the lack of the piano accompaniment part in the available sheet music prevented its inclusion in the Japanese edition. For this revised edition, however, the piano part has been reconstructed by transcribing from the 78 rpm recording of the orchestral performance in which Mr. Moyse played the solo, and it has made possible completion of *The Golden Age* both in name and in substance to my greatest joy. I would like to express my sincere gratitude to composer Yoshio Maruyama for his contribution to this transcription.

December 2008

Toshio Takahashi
In Matsumoto

作曲者紹介

セシル・シャミナード

　1857年8月8日パリに生まれ、1944年4月18日モンテカルロにて没す。数少ない女流作曲家でル・クーペ、サヴァール、マルシック、それにバンジャマン・ゴダールに学ぶ。18歳でピアニストとしてデビューし、以後フランス各地、イギリスに演奏旅行する傍ら、多数の魅力的なピアノ作品を書き、相当の人気を得たが、サロン風の音楽の域を出なかった。今でもよく演奏される有名な曲にヴァイオリンのための〈スペインのセレナード〉とフルートと管弦楽のための〈コンチェルティーノ〉Op.107（1902年）がある。シャミナードと懇意だったモイーズ先生によるとエレガントで美しいご夫人だったそうで、先生も特にコンチェルティーノには思い入れが深く、どこどこのパッセージをセシールはこのように歌っていた、などとなつかしそうに語りながらレッスンをしてくれたのが思い出される。

フレデリック・セゲール

　作品もフルートのための大幻想曲〈ガンの思い出〉しか現在残っていない。この作曲家の素性は全く不明であるが、1800年代後半、主にフランスを中心に活躍した、フルートのヴィルトゥオーソであり、作曲家であったと推測される。モイーズの名人芸の語り草になっているレコードが残っており、この曲をレッスンする折、モイーズ先生は一段と目を輝かせ、気合いたっぷりの若者のようであった。セゲールについて聞きそびれたのが惜しまれる。

ジュール・オーギュスト・ドゥメルスマン

　1833年にオランダに生まれ、1866年に33歳の若さで夭逝している。J.L.トゥルーに続くフランス楽派のL.ドゥルーと並ぶ代表的なフルート奏者である。

　わずか12歳の時にパリ音楽院で一等賞を得た。33年の生涯の大部分をパリで過ごしたが、師であるトゥルーをまねてベーム・フルートに頑固に反対したため、必要な資格はすべて備えていたにもかかわらず、パリ国立音楽院の教授に任命されなかった。彼はダブル・タンギングに優れ、いろいろな型のダブル・タンギングを披露したと言われている。大変奏曲"トレモロ"の最後の変奏曲でその名人芸の片鱗を窺うことができる。

　彼の出世作は〈オベロン幻想曲〉で、パリのパドルー演奏会の折は聴衆を熱狂させ、満場総立ちの喝采を受け「フルートのサラサーテ」と称された。この曲集に収められている2曲は彼の代表作で現在でもよく演奏されるが、膨大なカデンツァが至るところにあり、大変な難曲で吹き通すにはドゥメルスマン自身のような卓越したテクニックと強大なスタミナが必要である。

エドゥアール・ラロ

　1823年1月27日リルに生まれ、1892年4月22日にパリでなくなったスペインの血を引くフランスの作曲家。生地のリルでヴァイオリンとチェロを学び、1829年パリ国立音楽院で、ヴァイオリンと作曲を学んだ。しばらく弦楽四重奏団のヴィオラ奏者として活躍したが、1865年頃から作曲に転向し、1875年〈スペイン交響曲〉がサラサーテによって初演され成功を収める。1877年にはチェロ協奏曲で名声を不動のものにし、1882年にバレエ音楽〈ナムナ〉を作曲した。これは名舞踊家ニジンスキーを意識して書かれたもので、フルート・ソロの部分はそれまでの伝統的なテクニックでは演奏不能だったため、モイーズが低音のアタックの練習曲『Étude Exercise Technique』を書くきっかけとなった曲である。モイーズの演奏はニジンスキーを大いに感動させ、喜々として踊ったそうである。ラロの音楽はスペイン的な色彩感をもった大胆な楽想が特徴的で、当時のフランス音楽とは異なった情緒を持ち、特に〈ナムナ〉のオーケストレーションはダンディやドビュッシーに少なからず影響を与えた。

Profiles of Composers

Cécile Chaminade

Born in Paris on August 8, 1857, and died in Monte Carlo on April 18, 1944. One of rare female composers, she studied with Le Couppey, Savart, Marsick and Benjamin Godard. She made her debut as a pianist at the age of 18 and, while making concert tours in various parts of France and in Britain, she composed many attractive works for piano. These works won considerable popularity, but they were nothing more than salon music. Her well-known works which are played often even today include *Sérénade espagnole* and *Concertino*, op. 107 (1902). According to Maestro M. Moyse who was a good friend of Chaminade, she was an elegant beautiful lady. The maestro loved *Concertino* with a particular sentiment. I remember his telling me dearly during his lessons that Cécile had sung such and such passages in this way.

Frédéric Seghers

Grand fantasy *Souvenir de Gand* is the only work by Seghers remaining today. No biographical information is known of this composer, but he presumably was a virtuoso flutist-composer, who was active mainly in France during the second half of the 18th century. Maestro Moyse left us a fabulous recording of this work, often talked about as vividly evidencing his virtuosity. When he was teaching me how to play this piece, he looked like an ambitious young man with sparkling eyes, even more sparkling than usual. It is my regret that I asked nothing about Seghers himself.

Jules Auguste Demersseman

Born in 1833 in The Netherlands and died in 1866 at an age of only 33. He was a flutist representative of the French school, following Jean Louis Tulou and paralleled by Louis Dorus.

When he was only 12 years old, he won the first prize at the Paris Conservatory of Music. He lived in Paris almost all his 33 year life, but he was never appointed professor of the Paris Conservatory as he was firmly against the Boehm flute, even though he was fully qualified for the professorship. He was a master of double tonguing, and is said to have demonstrated many different ways of double tonguing. The final variation in *Grand Air Varié "Le Tremolo"* gives a glimpse of his virtuosity.

The work which made him famous was *Grande Fantaisie de Concert sur "Obéron" de Weber*. When it was performed in a Pasdeloup concert, the audience gave a standing ovation, and the composer came to be acclaimed the Sarasate of flute. The two compositions in this volume are representative of his works, and often performed even today, but they are made fabulously difficult by the tremendous cadenzas found everywhere in these works. Playing through either of the two works requires the kind of distinguished techniques and immense stamina which Demersseman himself had.

Edouard Lalo

A French composer with partly Spanish blood, who was born in Lille on January 27, 1823 and died in Paris on April 22, 1892. He learned to play the violin and the cello in his hometown Lille, and studied the violin and composition at the Paris Conservatory of Music to which he was admitted in 1829. For some time, he was active as the violist of a string quartet, but he switched to a composing career from around 1865, and his *Symphonie Espagnole* was successfully premiered by Sarasate in 1875. After his *Cello Concerto* established his fame in 1877, Lalo composed ballet music *Namouna* in 1882. He composed this work with the great dancer Vatzlav Nijinsky kept in mind. The flute solo part in this work was impossible to play by traditional techniques then known, and this difficulty provided the opportunity for Moyse to write *Etude Exercise Technique* to help flutists practice low voice attacks. The performance by Moyse deeply moved Nijinsky, who is said to have danced with great joy. Lalo's music is characterized by bold motifs with Spanish colorfulness, which differentiated his works from most other works of French music at the time. Especially, the orchestration of *Namouna* gave no little influence on Vincent d'Indy and Claude Debussy.

<h2 style="text-align:center;">本書の記号の意味と注意
Points to be Noted for Users of This Collection</h2>

フルート・パートにおけるブレス記号について
Breathing signs in the flute part:

, 　常に必要、フレーズの音楽的表現上しばしば不可欠である。
　　Breathing always necessary, often indispensable for the musical expression of the phrase.

(') 　音楽的には良いが、必ずしも必要ではない。
　　Breathing musically acceptable, but not always necessary.

V 　表情的ブレス、音楽的フレーズをより表情豊かにする。
　　Expressive breathing, making the musical phrase more expressive.

(V) 　できたら避けるべきで、ブレスしてもすばやく行われるべきである。
　　Should be avoided whenever possible; if inevitable, the breathing should be quick.

その他の表情記号について
Other expression marks:

- 　短い表情的強調
　Short expressive emphasis

— 　長い表情的強調
　Long expressive emphasis

急激なものではなく、柔らかさ、暖かさをもって表現されるときに最も効果的である。
Most effective in soft and warm expressions, not abrupt ones.

> 　軽い表情アクセントで、くずれたバランスを立て直すのに有効。
　Light expressive accent, effective for restoring a lost balance.

< 　強い表情アクセント。感動を腹の底からつぎ込むような力強い表現。
　Strong expressive accent for powerful expression as if to pour a whole emotion from the bottom of its source.

●ゴールデン・エージ *Vol. 3* ──────目次
Golden Age of the Flutists vol.3

- Contents -

Concertino
pour flûte
avec accompagnement de piano

Cécile Chaminade, Op.107

sempre molto sostenuto
poco string.
cresc.
poco string.
cresc.
B
a tempo
a tempo
f
mf
poco string.
cresc.
p
f
cresc.
p
sf
f
sf
f

ff
f
C Più animato
agitato
Più animato
f
mf marcato
p
Stringendo
Stringendo

E
p f
marcato
dolce
mf
p
f
f
sempre f
mf
Stringendo
Stringendo
F
ff
f
mf

mf
p
rall.
espress.
rall.
p
sempre rall.
pp
sempre rall.
dim.
G a Tempo
a Tempo
p
p
legg.
3
3   3   3   3   3
f
f

I
tr
p
mf
cresc.
non legato
f
ff
J
marcatissimo
ff
f
3
mf
cresc.
f
tr
marcatissimo
f
mf
f
mf
cresc.

K
ff
f
mf
p
rall.
rall. molto
p espress.
p
rall.
rall. molto
dim.
pp
pp
ppp
mf
rall.
ten.
ten.

ten.
pp
L
Tempo I
pp
Tempo I
pp
3
3
3
f
3
3
p
3
3
3
3
p
3
3
3
poco string.
cresc.
6
7
7
7
6
poco string.
cresc.
tr

M
a tempo
f
a tempo
mf
cresc.
poco string.
a tempo
f
a tempo
f
6
6
sempre f
f
ff
3
poco allarg.
3

N
Presto
f
Presto
sfp
tr
Ossia
8va
O
poco rit.
accel.
accel.
8va
f
8va
tr
cresc.
ff
tr
poco allarg.
poco allarg.
8va
ff
p
p

Souvenir de Gand

Grande Fantaisie pour flûte

Frédéric Seghers

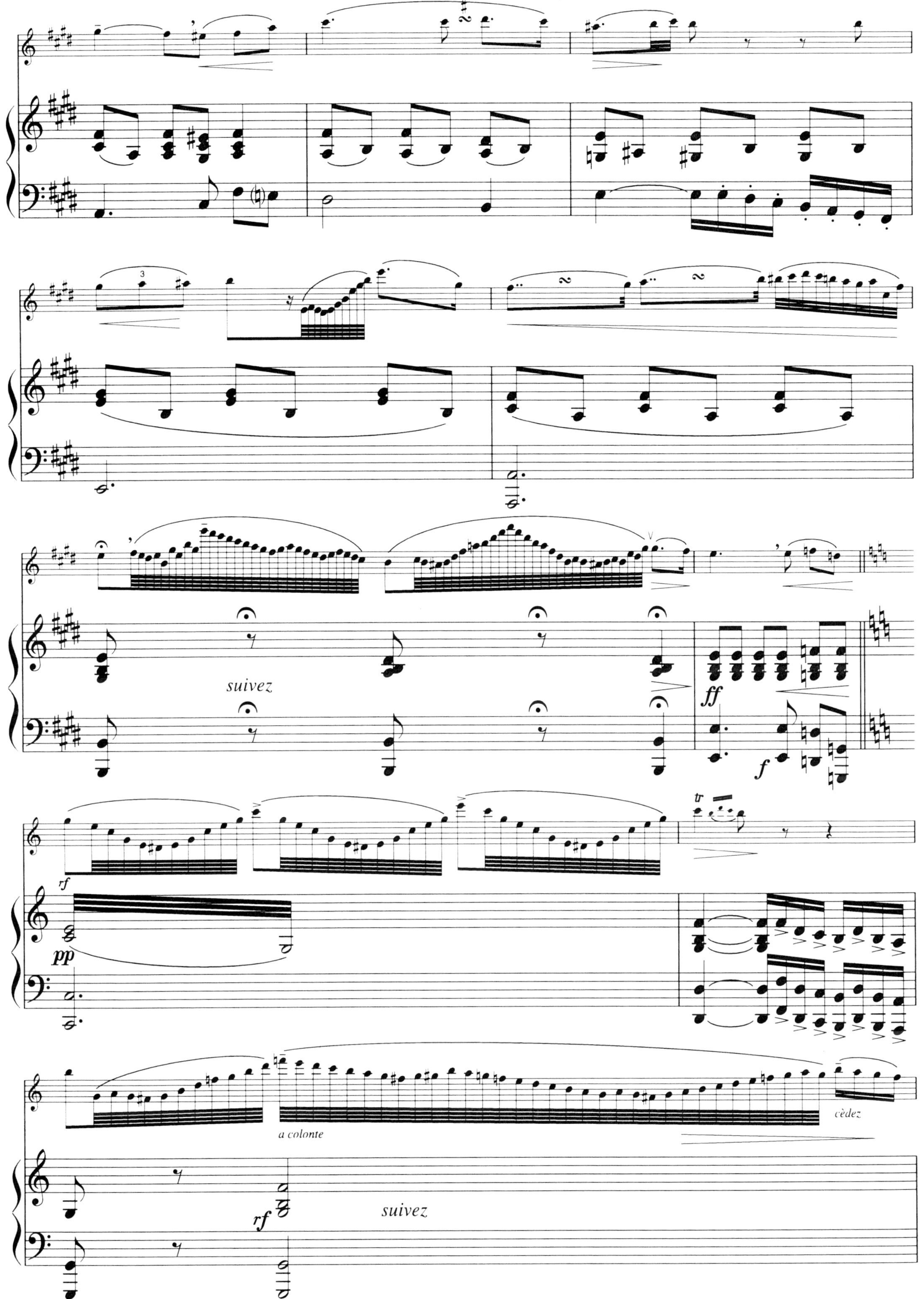
suivez
ff
f
rf
pp
tr
a colonte
cèdez
rf
suivez

a tempo
pp
a tempo
un peu animé
rf
p
cresc.
mp
diminuez toujours
tr
enchainez
f
p
pp
ff
THÈME
Allegretto
pp
Allegretto
ppp
f

p
cresc.
sonore
mf
p
large
rit.
1.
2.
bien chante
rall.
p
ff
ff
ff plus vite

1ère VAR.
Allegretto
p bien chanté
Allegretto
pp
cresc.
p
cresc.
plein son
mf
f

1.
2.
ff
8va
plus vite
8va
2me VAR.
Moderato
f
Moderato
pp
p
rf
ff
p

très léger.
stacc.
cresc.
dim.
rit.
stacc.
ff
tr
long
rapide
f
ppp
cresc.
ff
lento
pressez peu à peu
p
cresc.
rall.
très vivement et brillant
ten.
a tempo
grand dim.
rf
a tempo

p
rf
cresc.
tutti
ff
3 3 3 3
3 3 3
3

3me VAR.
Allegretto
p
cresc.
Allegretto
pp
p
cresc.
f
sonore
mf
sonore

f
ff
rf
rf
rf
rf
rf
3
3
3
3
3
sec.

Andante
con espressione
p
Andante
con espressione
pp
3 3 3
mf
cresc.
sonore
5 rit.
rf
p
un peu plus vite
un peu plus vite
mf
rf
p delicat
pp
pp

plus vite
rf
rf
rf
p
stacc.
pp
ppp una corda
à volonte
tr
3
f
Allegretto
p
Allegretto
pp

mf
suivez
rall.
un peu plus vite
un peu plus vite
p
pp subito
pp una corda
pp
pp
pp

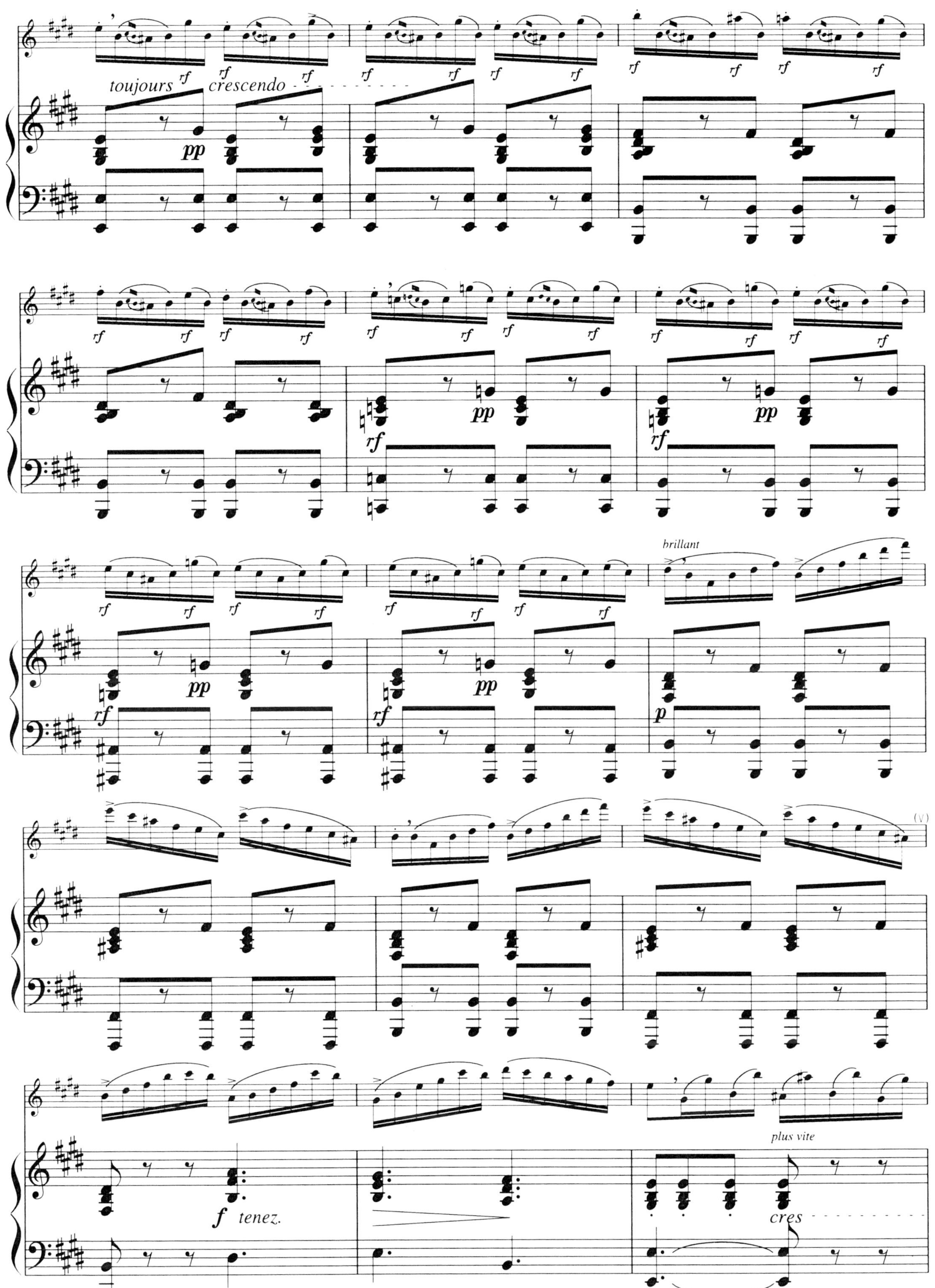

toujours rf crescendo
pp
rf rf rf rf rf rf rf rf rf rf rf
rf rf rf rf rf rf rf rf rf rf rf rf
pp pp
rf rf
brillant
pp pp
rf rf p
(V)
plus vite
f tenez.
cres

cen
do
f
cres
cen
do
ff
fff
ff

Grande Fantaisie de Concert

sur "Obéron" de Weber

pour flûte et piano

Jules Demersseman, Op.52

Allegro marziale

Un peu animé
fz
p
mf
Un peu animé
p
cresc.
a tempo
pp
dim.
rall.
a tempo
cresc.
a tempo
rall.
a tempo
pp
p
p
ff
p
f
mf
p
cresc.
ff
V
rall.
fff
rall.
3
Suivez
f
p
pp

cresc.
mf
cresc.
mf
toujours cresc.
cresc.
cresc.
Très vite
ff
pp
dim.
ff
MAJEUR
a tempo
pp
a tempo
ppp

ppp
rall.
rall.
Andante non troppo lento
ff
THÈME
pp dolce
con espress.
rall.
a tempo
ppp
p
mp
p

mf
mp
Un peu animé
fz
dim.
fz
fz
Un peu animé
a tempo
dim. e rit.
ppp
a tempo
dim. et suivre
ppp
rall.
a tempo
dim.
con espress.
rall.
a tempo
f
ff
Ped.

VAR.
Même Mouvt
Même Mouvt
p
mp
cresc.
mf
pp
mf
fz
mf
f
cresc.
p
mf
ff brillante
mf
mf
f
mf
cresc.
cresc.

Même Mouvt (à (à 4 temps)
f
ff
pp
ff
3
Même Mouvt (à 4 temps)
f
mf
pp
ff
pp
ff
sempre ff
pp
f
3
pp
ff
3
1.
2.
3
3
1.
2.
f
f

Mouvt du Thème
tutti
pp
Andante
f
grave
Andante
mf
gliss.
pp

rall.
a tempo
ff
rall.
a tempo
3
3
pp
pp
rall.
rall.
f
p
a tempo
f
a tempo
f

Animato poco a poco
p
cresc.
Animato poco a poco
p
cresc.
CADENZA
rit.
long
passionato
cresc.
rit.
f
cresc.
ppp
pp
mf
p
mf
p
p
mf
f
ff
pp
ff
pp
long
Simple coup de langue

rall.
Double coup de langue
Simple coup de langue
ff
FINAL
Allegro
Allegro
f brillante
3

f
tr
3
( )
tr
tr tr tr tr tr tr
Allegro vivace
p
Allegro vivace
loure
cresc.
pp
f
pp
f
f
pp
pp

loure
f

Grand Air Varié "Le Tremolo"

pour flûte et piano

tr
tr
tr
pp
cresc.
genereux
pp
poco cresc.
(très vite)
cresc. e animato
p
mf
long
Vite
f
pp
f
pp
p espress.
mf animato e cresc.
poco cresc.
rall.
rall.
pp
p
mf
con fuoco
f
pp
ff

à volonté
rall.
THÈME
Allegretto
pp
pp
p
mf
dim.
Allegretto
pp
p
mf
tr
pp
p
mf
bien chanté
p
cresc.
p
cresc.
mf
cresc.
p
cresc.
f

souple
p
pp
p
mf
dim.
Tutti
cresc.
mf
cresc.
ff
ff
1ère VAR.
p
Plus lent
pp
cresc.
Plus lent
pp
ff
p
ff
p
cresc.

f
p
mp
3 3 3 3 3 3
p
p
ff
p
ff
f
mf
p
pp
5
cresc.
tr tr tr tr
souple, un peu retenu
a tempo
5
p
cresc.

rall.
en retenant
ff
p
mf
pp
f
pp
tr tr tr
f
Lent
ff
Tempo I
pp
p
p
cresc.
Tempo I
pp
ff
p
p
f
p
p
ff
p
f
ff
ff
Tutti
ff

Adagio
pp
gliss.
ppp
Adagio
pp
ppp
rall.
a volonte
pp
cresc.
p
rall.
p
pp
cresc.
fz
p

allarg.
tr
Largement
large et sonore
soutenu
son plein
allarg.
Largement
ff
mf
mf
rall.
a tempo
tr
pp
mf
con fuoco
a tempo
pp
mf
pp
mf
ff
m.g.
8va
Serrez le mouvt
tr   tr   tr   tr
pp e cresc.
Serrez le mouvt
pp

rall.
Vite
long
lent et de plus en plus vite
rit.
ppp
avec force
ff f mf p
f
Tempo I
pp
gliss.
ppp
Tempo I
pp
ppp
rall.
a volonte
p
3
3
rall.
p
pp
rall.
fff
pppp
tr
tr
tr
tr
f
pp
Allegro
Tutti
8va
f cresc.
6
6

8va
p
fz
fz
FINAL
p
Un poco lento
Un poco lento
pp
cresc.
cresc.

cresc.
mf
dim. et cèdez légèrement
Suivez
a tempo
a tempo
p
cresc.
cresc.
dim.
dim.
p
cresc.
pp
cresc.

toujours cresc.
f
f
ff
ff

Namouna
Ballet en 2 actes - Solo de flûte
avec accompagnement de piano

Edouard Lalo
Reduction for piano by Yoshio Maruyama

cresc.
f
animez
animez
léger cédez
subito pp
léger cédez
p
animez
animez
cresc.
élargir
f
rit.
a tempo
rit.
rit.
a tempo
rit.
p
a tempo
ff
cédez
rit.
a tempo
mf
cédez
rit.

rit.
a tempo
rit.
a tempo
pp
poco a poco
rit.
a tempo
rit.
a tempo
poco a poco
pp
accelerando
accelerando
pp
(♪=116)
(♪=116)
pp
cresc.
p
animez
animez
tr
ff
cresc.
f
sf
sf

演奏会用フルート名曲集

ゴールデンエージ　3　　　　　　　　●

編者 ————————————	マルセル・モイーズ
監修 ————————————	高橋利夫
第 1 版第 1 刷発行 ————————	2008年12月15日
第 1 版第 9 刷発行 ————————	2023年 9 月25日
発行 ————————————	株式会社全音楽譜出版社
————————————————	東京都新宿区上落合2丁目13番3号〒161-0034
————————————————	TEL・営業部03・3227-6270
————————————————	出版部03・3227-6280
————————————————	URL　http://www.zen-on.co.jp/
————————————————	ISBN978-4-11-509004-0

複写・複製・転載等厳禁　Printed in Japan

2309074

Edited by M. Moyse & T. Takahashi

The Golden Age of the Flutists

マルセル・モイーズ／髙橋利夫　編

演奏会用フルート名曲集
ゴールデン・エージ（全 3 巻）

The Golden Age of the Flutists Vol. 1
ゴールデン・エージ　1　　（ed. M.Moyse / T.Takahashi）

The Golden Age of the Flutists Vol. 2
ゴールデン・エージ　2　　（ed. M.Moyse / T.Takahashi）

The Golden Age of the Flutists Vol. 3
ゴールデン・エージ　3　　（ed. M.Moyse / T.Takahashi）

THE GOLDEN AGE OF THE FLUTISTS VOL.3

Chosen and revised by Marcel Moyse
Supervised by Toshio Takahashi

演奏会用フルート名曲集

ゴールデン・エージ 3

マルセル・モイーズ──編　髙橋利夫──監修

Flute Part

zen-on music

● ゴールデン・エージ *Vol. 3* ─────目次

Golden Age of the Flutists vol.3

- Flute Part

- Contents -

Concertino

pour flûte et orchestre (*ou* piano)

Cécile Chaminade, Op.107

5
ff
C Più animato, agitato
f
stringendo
p
tr
cresc.
tr
D
cresc.
f
f
cresc.
f
E
f
p
p

dolce
f
sempre f
stringendo
F
ff
mf
rall.
espress.
sempre rall.
pp
G a tempo
p
legg.
f
f
tr
p
cresc.

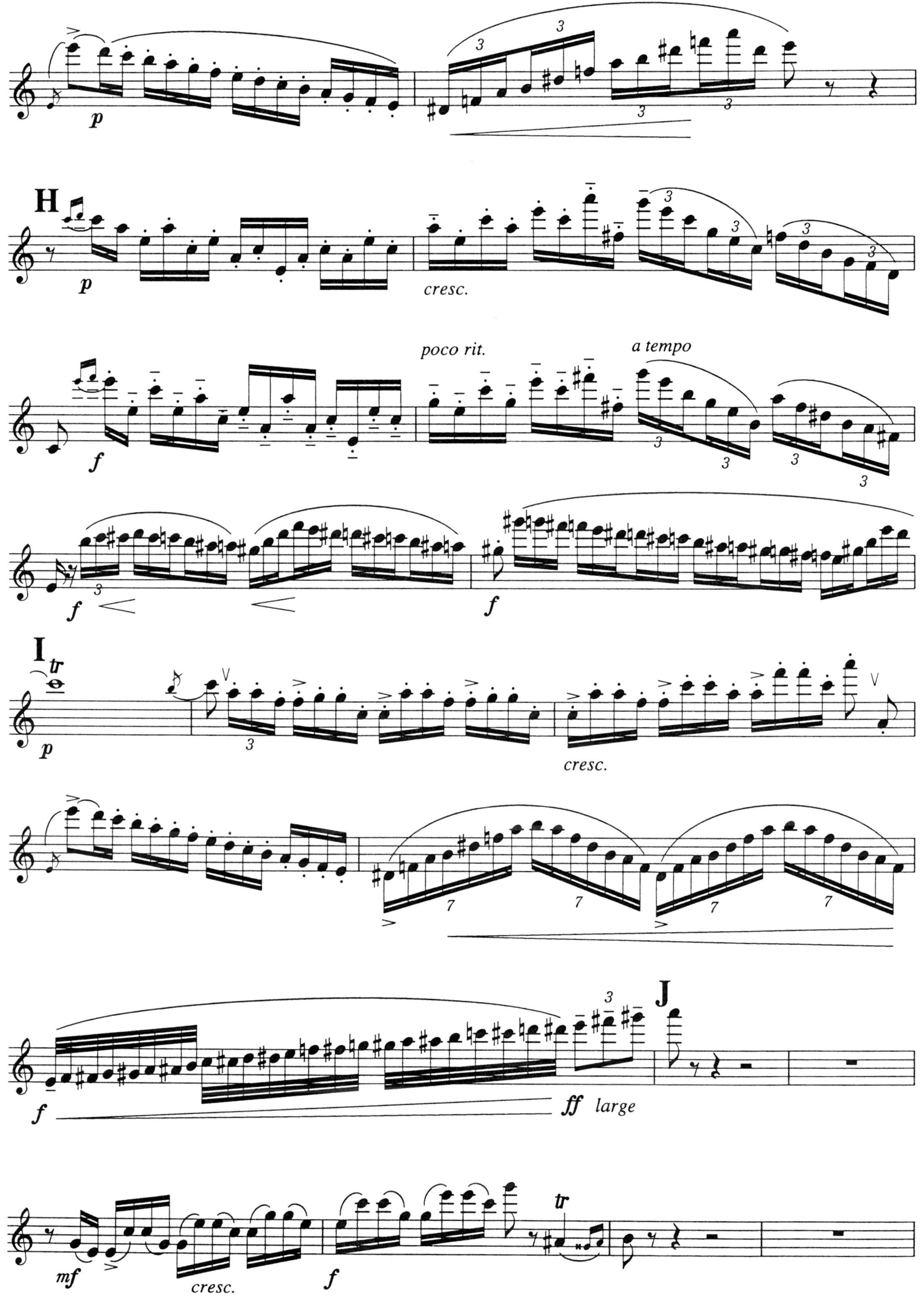
7
H
p
cresc.
poco rit.
a tempo
f
f
f
I
tr
p
cresc.
7
7
7
7
J
f
ff large
mf
cresc.
f
tr

largando
K
ff
f
mf
3
rit. molto
p espress.
serrez
rit.
pp
long.
pp léger
ppp
3
rall.
mf
rall.
3
ten.
ten.
ten.

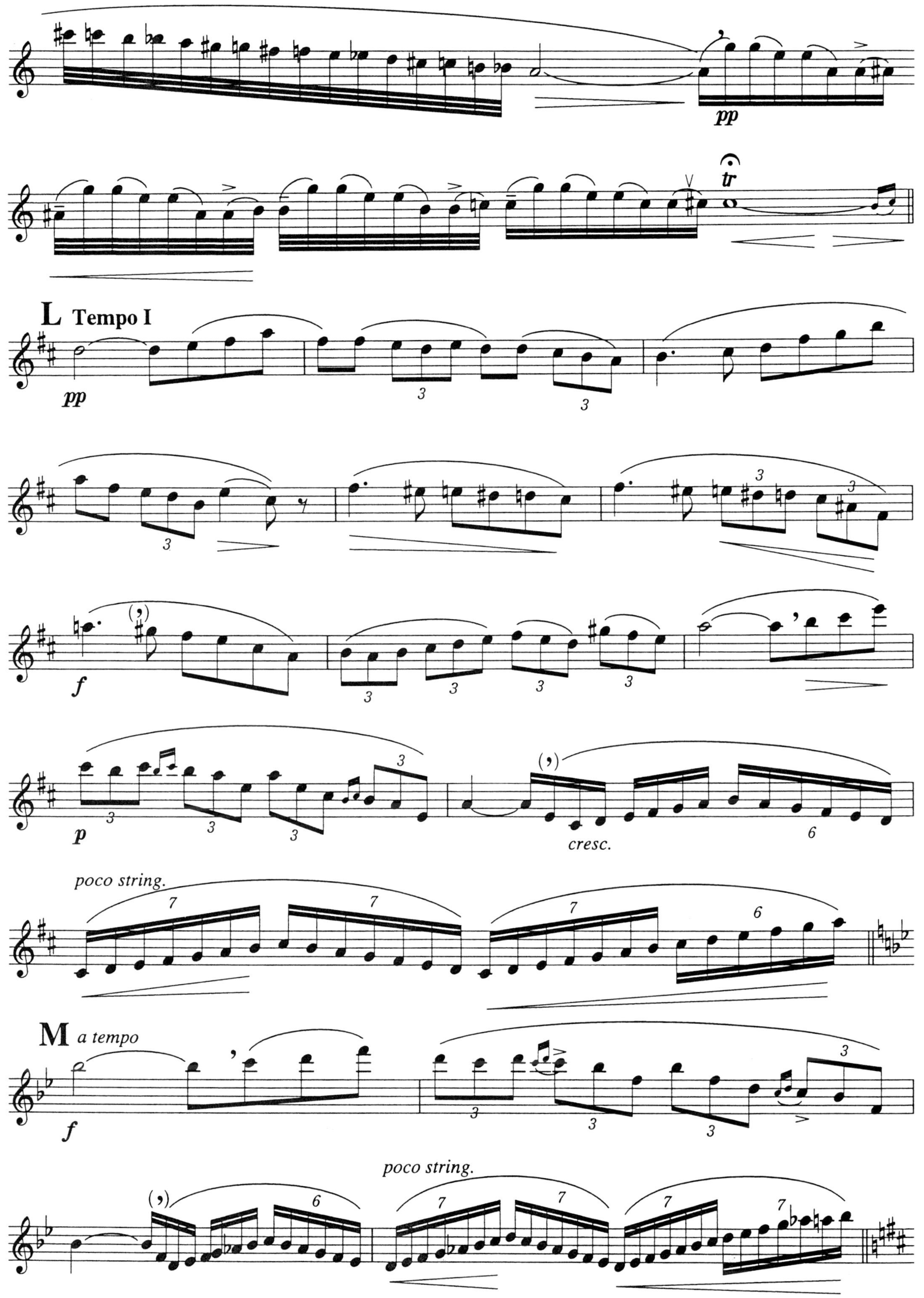
pp
tr
L Tempo I
pp
3
3
3
3
f
3
3
3
3
p
3
3
3
cresc.
6
poco string.
7
7
7
6
M a tempo
3
f
3
3
poco string.
6
7
7
7
7

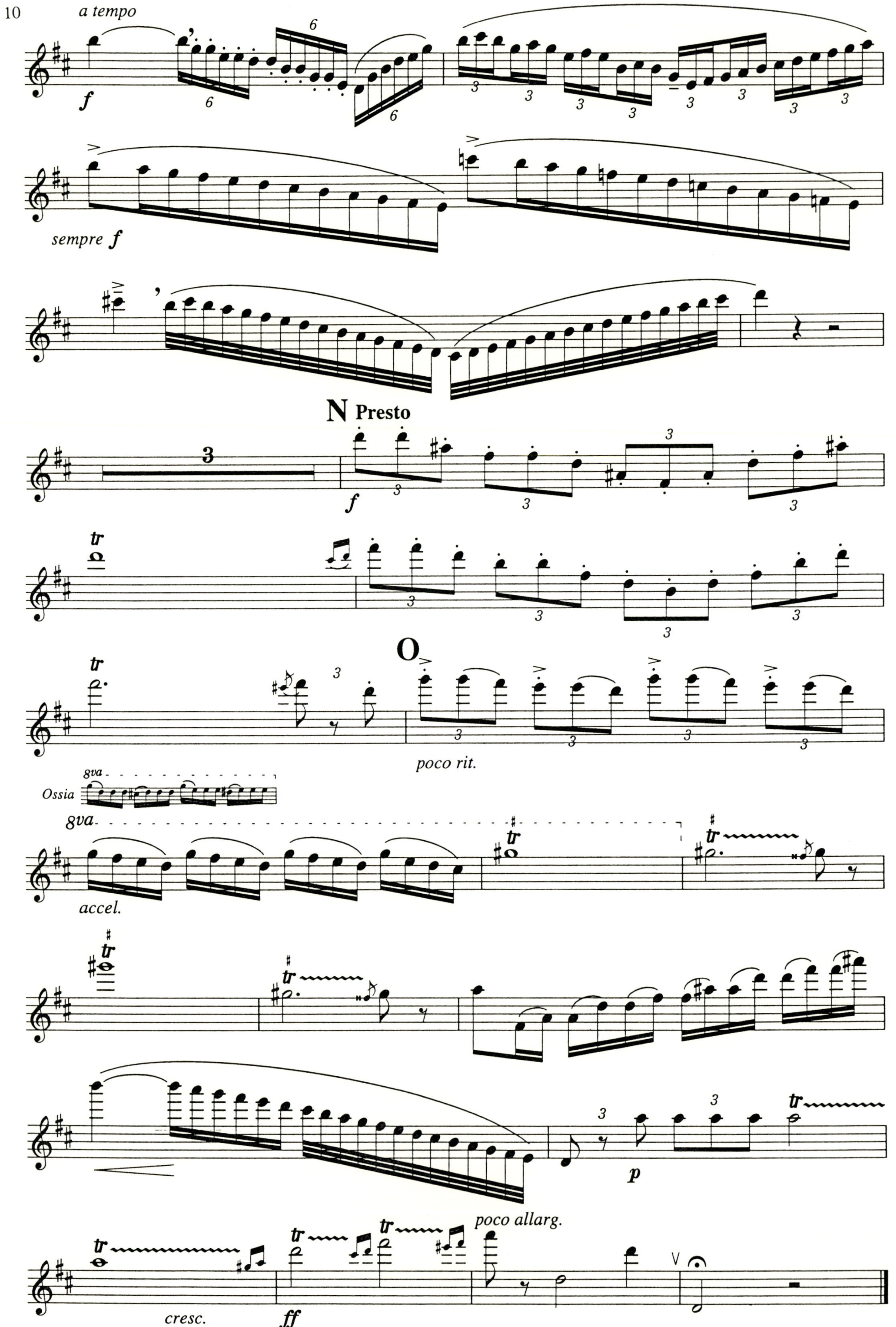

a tempo
f
sempre f
N Presto
f
tr
tr
O
poco rit.
Ossia
8va.
8va.
accel.
tr
tr
tr
tr
3
p
poco allarg.
tr
tr
tr
cresc.
ff

•

Souvenir de Gand
Grande Fantaisie pour flûte

Frédéric Seghers

a tempo
pp
rf
un peu animé
p
3 3 3 3 3 3
cresc.
3 3
mp
p
pp
tr
enchainez
f
6/8
THÈME
Allegretto
6/8
pp
p
cresc.
sonore
mf
bien chanté
large
rit.
1.
2.
8
6/8

1ère VAR.
Allegretto
p bien chanté
3 3 3 3 3
cresc.
p
cresc.
plein son
mf
f
1.
2.
2me VAR.
Moderato
8
f
3 3
p

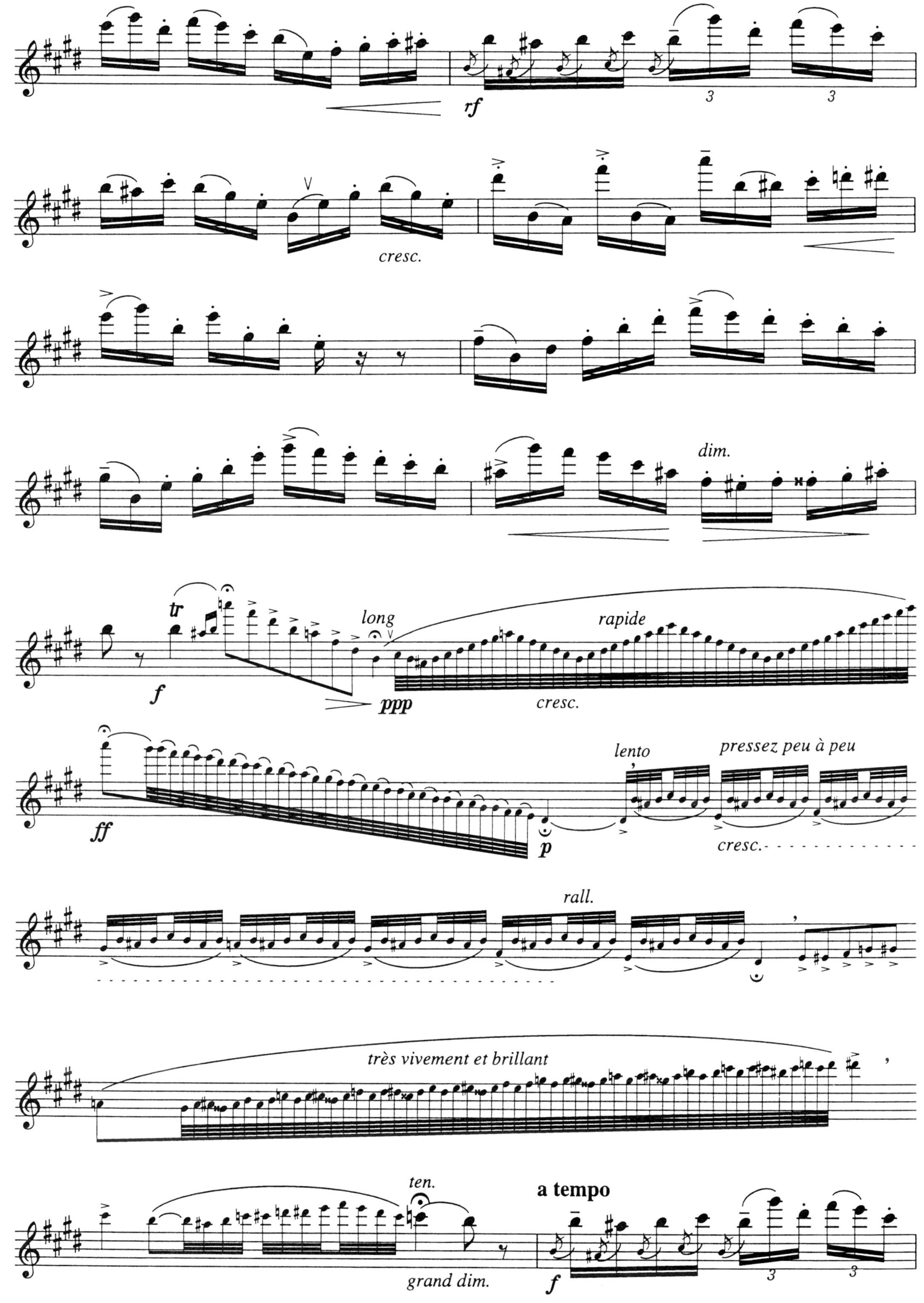
rf
cresc.
dim.
tr
long
rapide
f
ppp
cresc.
ff
lento
pressez peu à peu
p
cresc.- - - - - - - - - -
rall.
très vivement et brillant
ten.
a tempo
grand dim.
f

p
rf
cresc.
3   3
8
6/8
3me VAR.
Allegretto
6/8
p
cresc. - -
- - - en - - - - - - do
p
cresc. - - - - - - - -
f
sonore

sonore
21
Andante
con espressione
p
f
3
3
mf
3
5
rit.
cresc.
sonore
un peu plus vite
3
3
mf
rf
p délicat
plus vite
rf

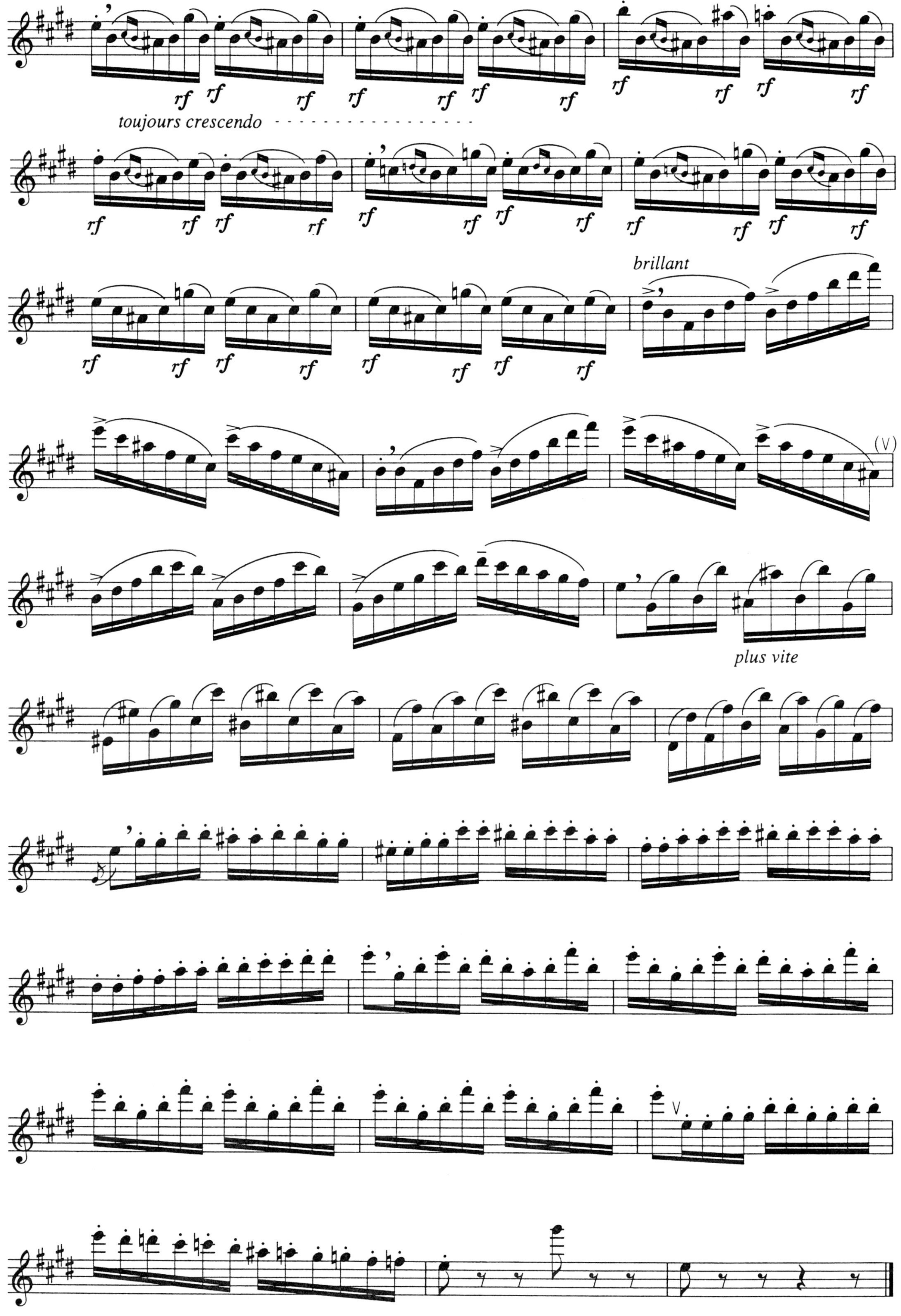
rf rf rf rf rf rf rf rf rf rf rf
toujours crescendo
rf rf rf rf rf rf rf rf rf rf rf rf
brillant
rf rf rf rf rf rf rf rf
(V)
plus vite

Grande Fantaisie de Concert

sur "Obéron" de Weber

pour flûte et piano

Jules Demersseman, Op.52

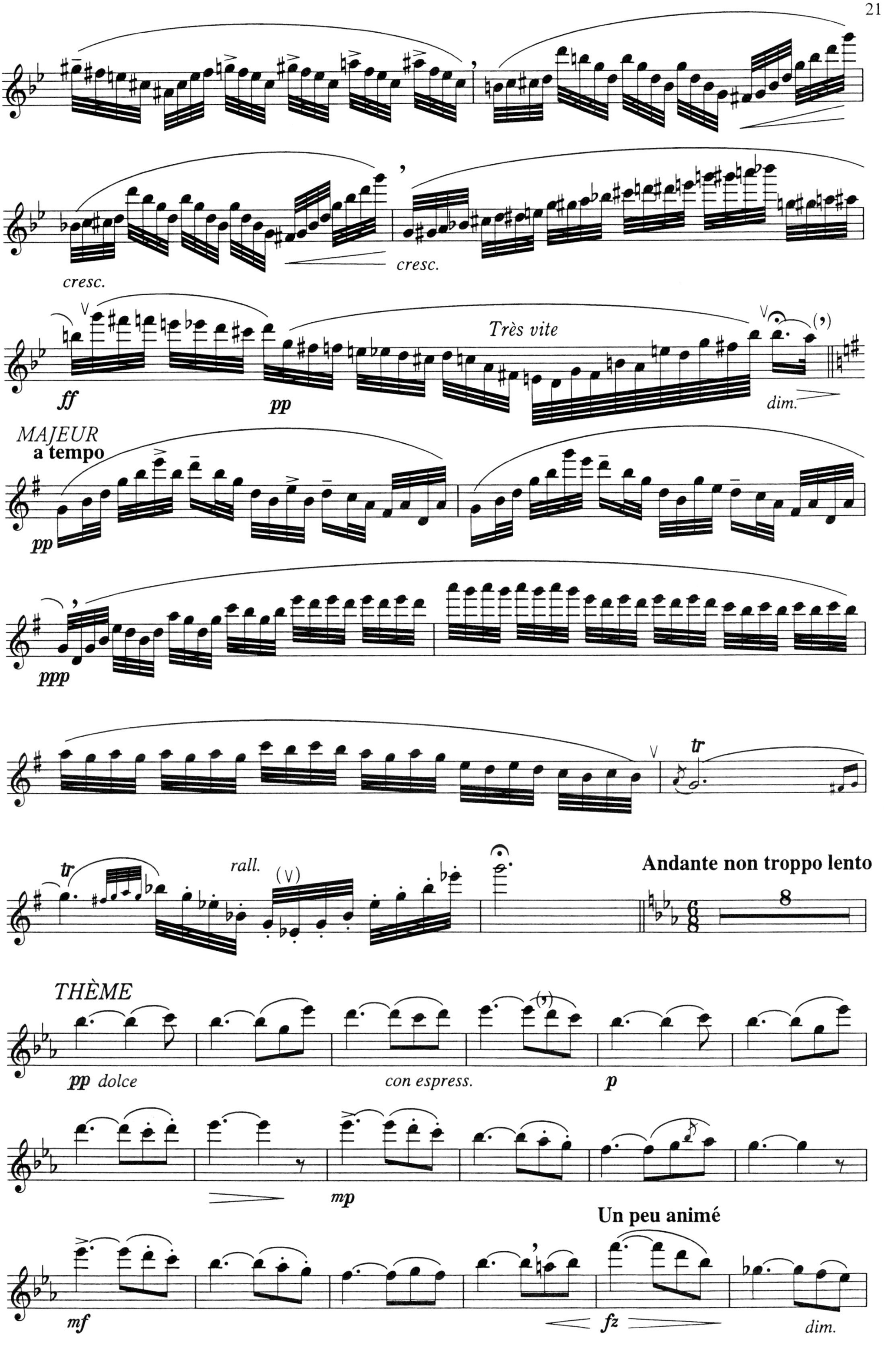
cresc.
cresc.
ff
pp
Très vite
dim.
MAJEUR
a tempo
pp
ppp
tr
tr
rall.
(V)
Andante non troppo lento
8
THÈME
pp dolce
con espress.
p
mp
Un peu animé
mf
fz
dim.

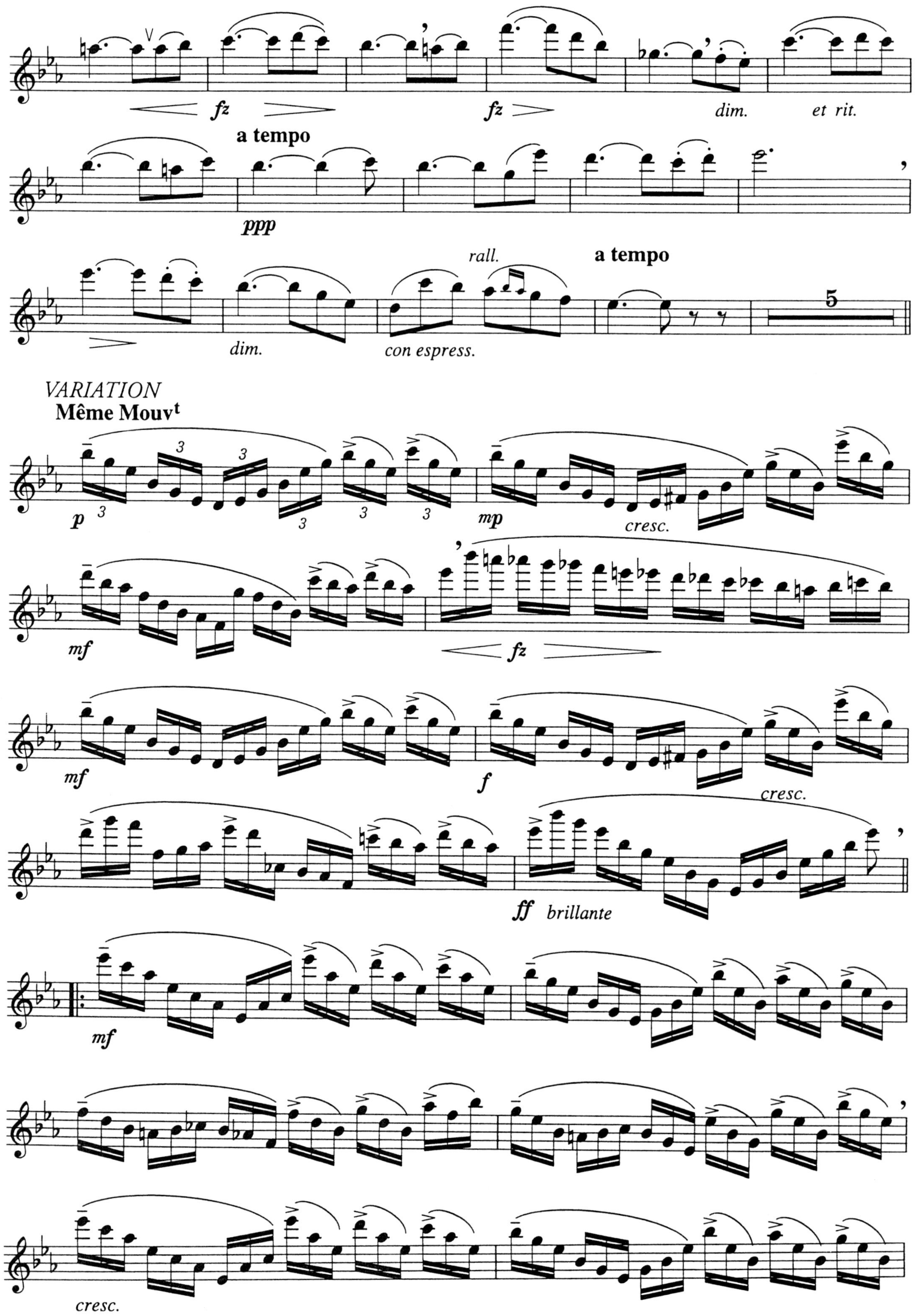

22
fz
dim. et rit.
a tempo
ppp
rall.
a tempo
5
dim.
con espress.
VARIATION
Même Mouv^t
p
3
3
3
3
3
3
mp
cresc.
mf
fz
mf
f
cresc.
ff brillante
mf
cresc.

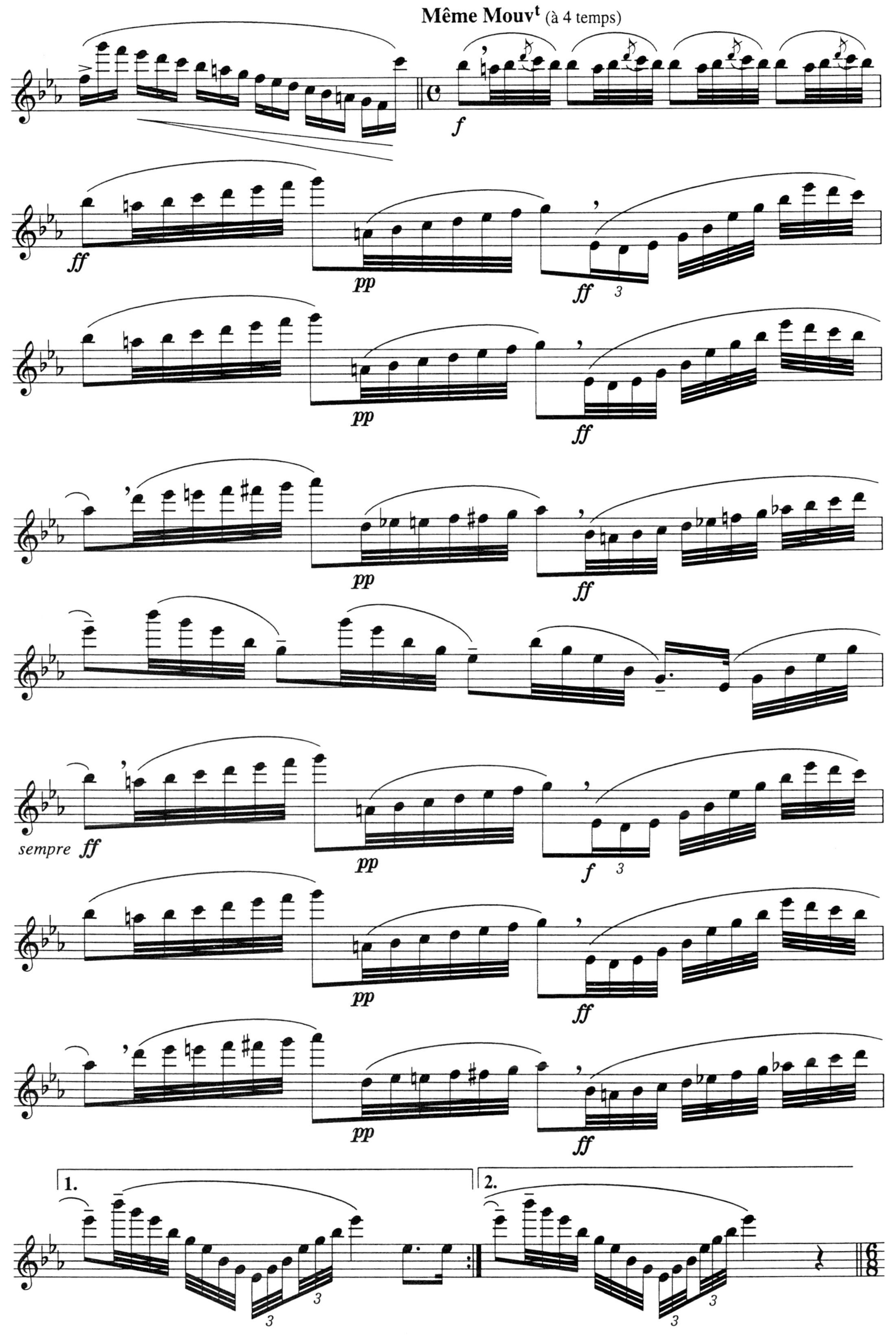

Même Mouvᵗ (à 4 temps)
f
ff
pp
ff
3
pp
ff
pp
ff
sempre ff
pp
f
3
pp
ff
pp
ff
1.
2.
3
3
3
6
8

Mouv.t du Thème
Andante
13
f
grave
gliss.
pp
rall.
a tempo
ff
3
3
rf large
pp
rall.
a tempo
f
Animato poco a poco
p
cresc.

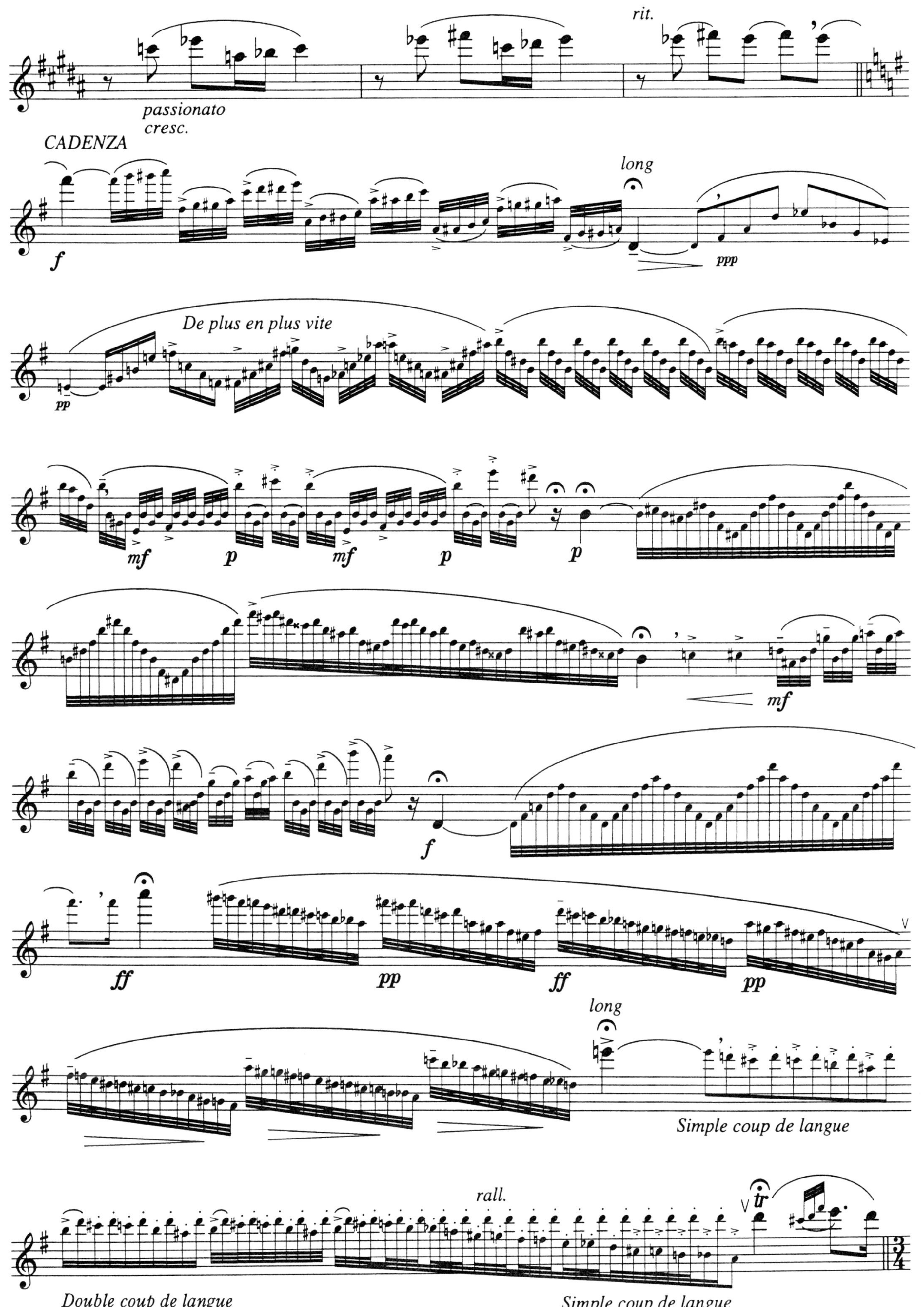
rit.
passionato
cresc.
CADENZA
long
f
ppp
De plus en plus vite
pp
mf
p
mf
p
p
mf
f
ff
pp
ff
pp
long
Simple coup de langue
rall.
tr
Double coup de langue
Simple coup de langue

FINAL
Allegro

f
tr
3
tr
tr
tr tr tr tr tr tr
Allegro vivace
p
cresc.
pp
cresc.
ff

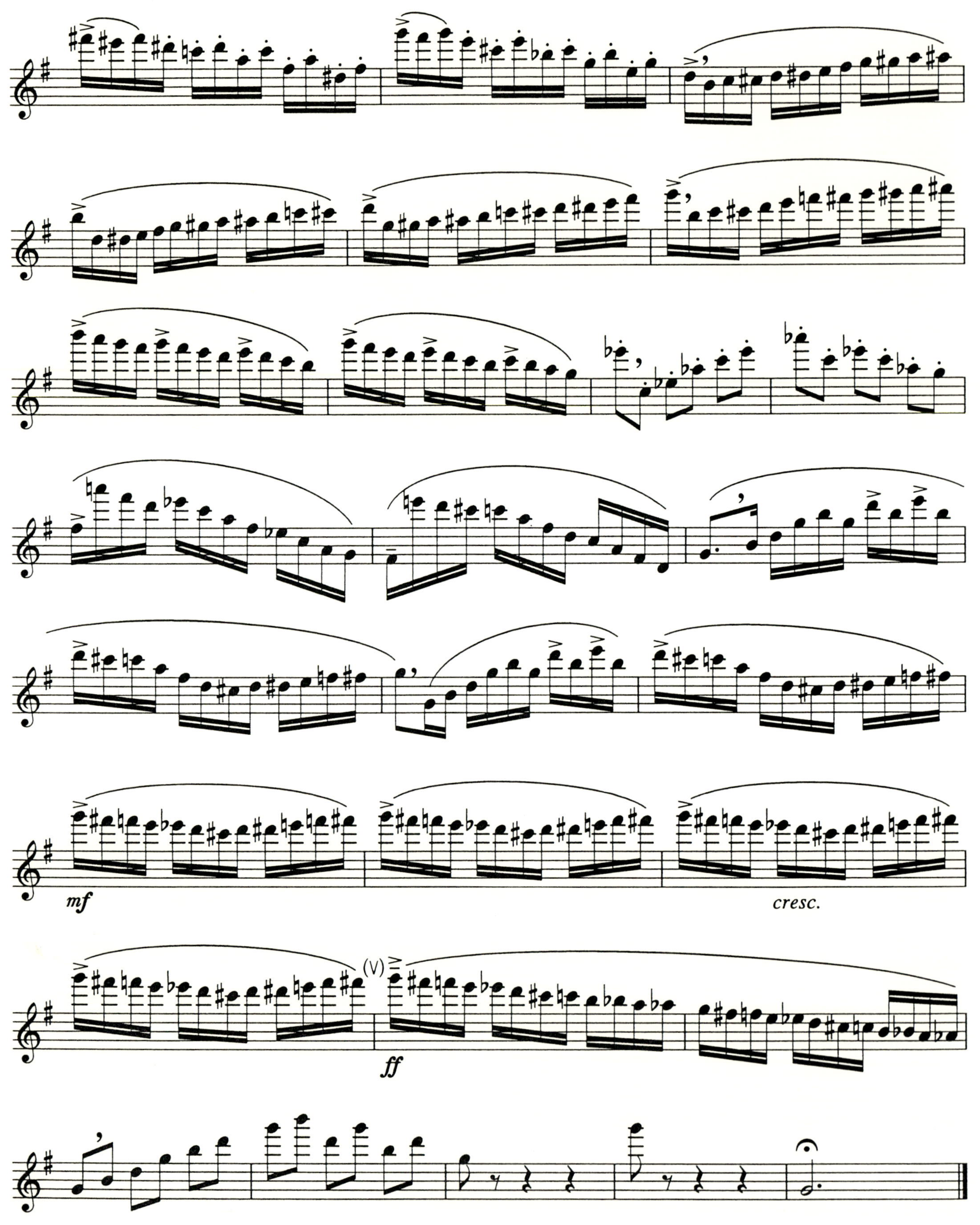

mf
cresc.
(V)
ff

●

Grand Air Varié "Le Tremolo"

pour flûte et piano

Jules Demersseman, Op.3

mf
con fuoco
f
pp
THÈME
Allegretto
à volonté
tr
La petite note MI très claire
pp
p
mf
dim.
pp
p
mf
bien chanté
p
cresc.
mf
cresc.
p
p
mf
dim.
souple
tr
tr
tr
tr
tr
tr
p
mf
cresc.
1ère VAR.
Plus lent
7
p
3
3
3
3
p
3
3
3
3
pp
3
3
3
3
3
cresc.

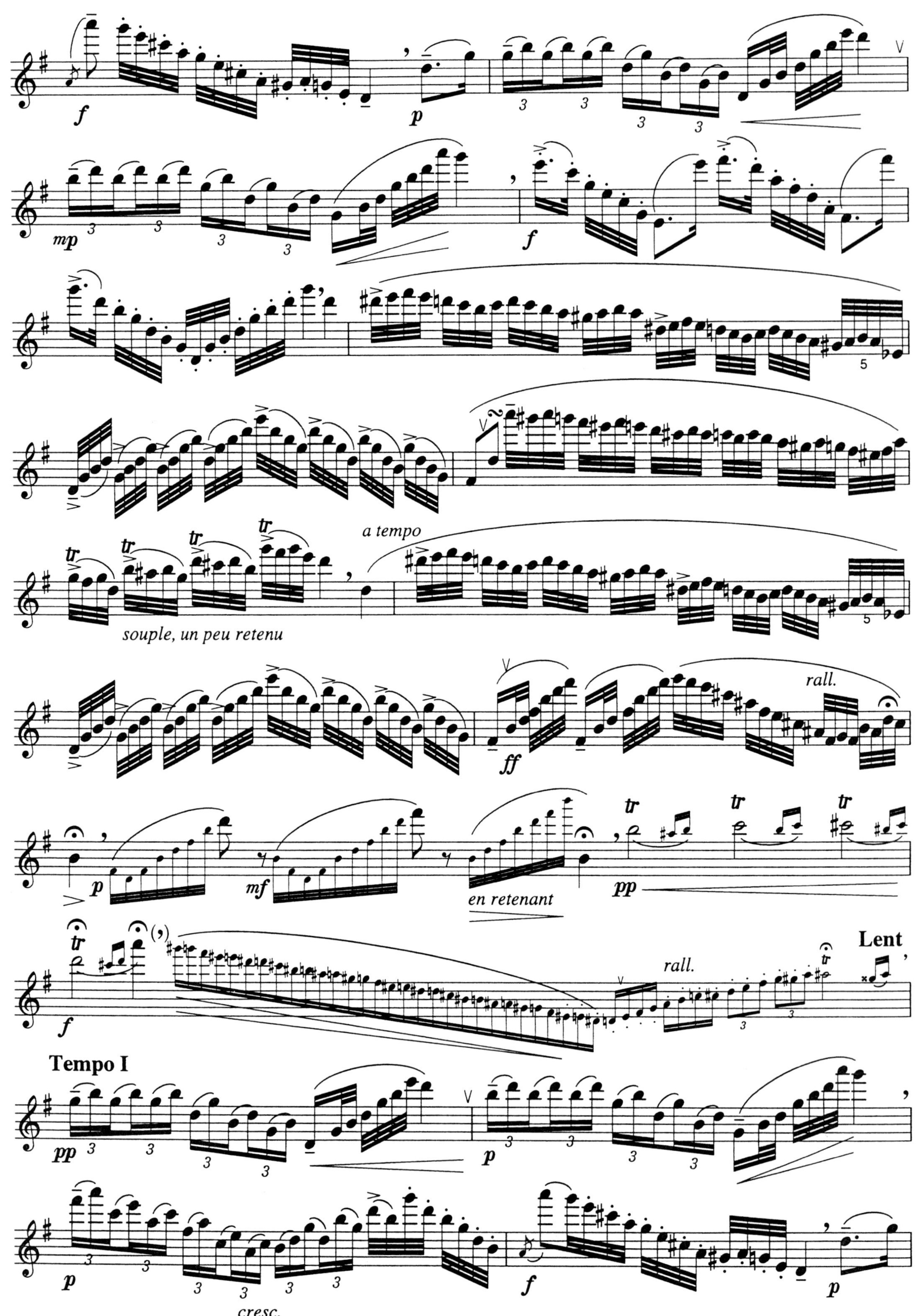

f
p
3 3
3 3
mp
3 3
3 3
f
5
a tempo
tr tr tr tr
souple, un peu retenu
5
ff
rall.
p
mf
en retenant
pp
tr tr tr
f
rall.
Lent
tr (᾿)
3 3
Tempo I
pp
3 3
3 3
p
3 3
p
3 3 3 3
f
p
cresc.

3 3
3 3
p 3 3 3 3
ff
Adagio
12
pp
ppp
gliss.
rall.
à volonté
dim.
p 3 3 pp cresc.
allarg.
tr Largement
large et sonore 3 3 3 soutenu son plein
rall.
3
a tempo
tr
pp mf con fuoco
f 3 3
Serrez le mouvᵗ
tr tr tr tr
pp e cresc.
long
rall. Vite
long
lent et de plus en plus vite rit.
ppp avec force ff f mf p

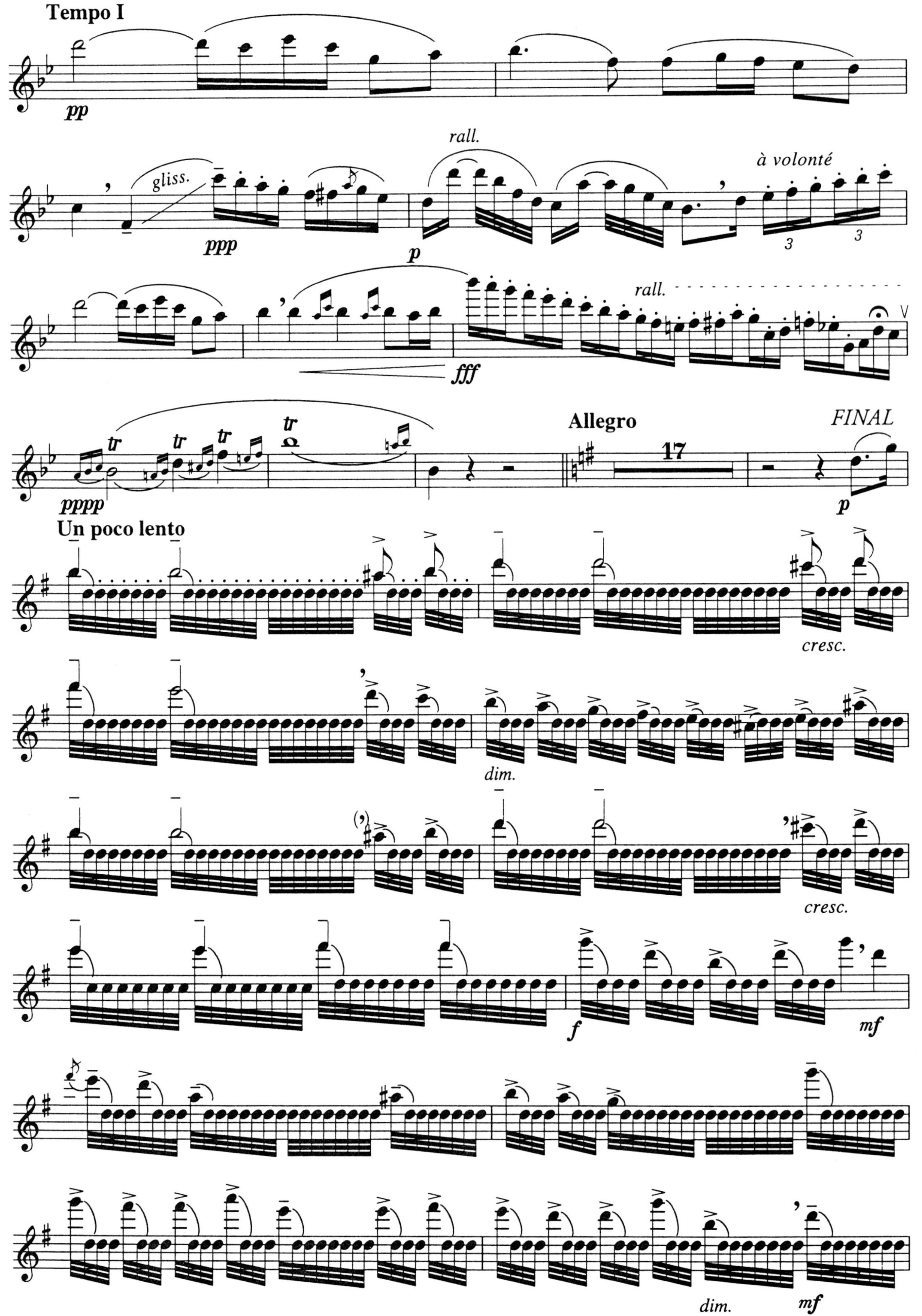
Tempo I
pp
rall.
gliss.
à volonté
ppp
p
3 3
p
rall.
fff
tr tr tr tr
pppp
Allegro
17
FINAL
p
Un poco lento
cresc.
dim.
cresc.
f
mf
dim. mf

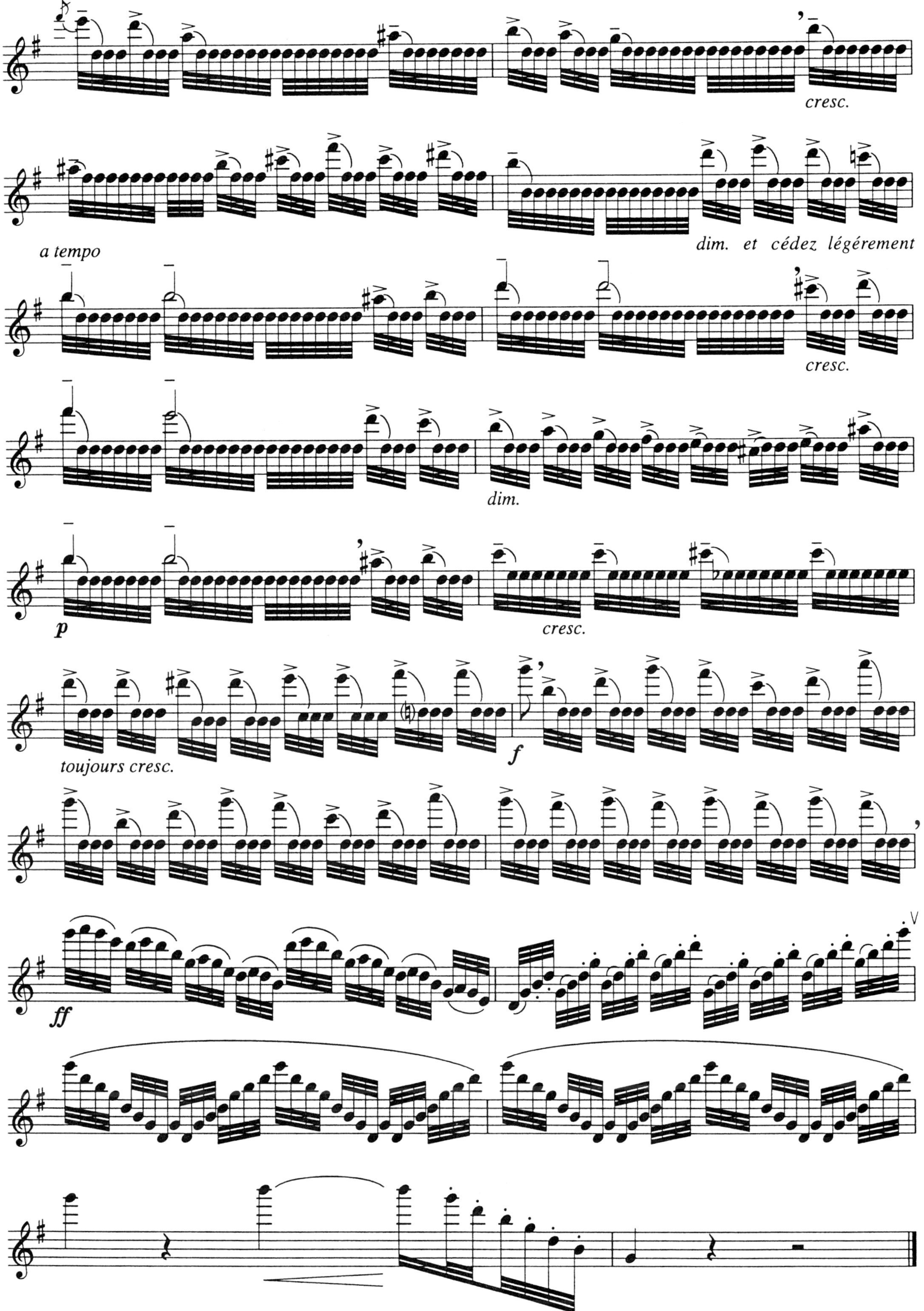

cresc.
a tempo
dim. et cédez légérement
cresc.
dim.
p
cresc.
toujours cresc.
f
ff

Namouna

Ballet en 2 actes - Solo de flûte

avec accompagnement de piano

Edouard Lalo

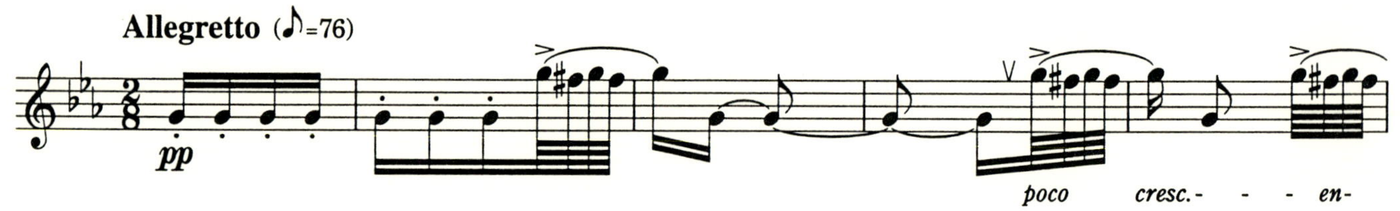

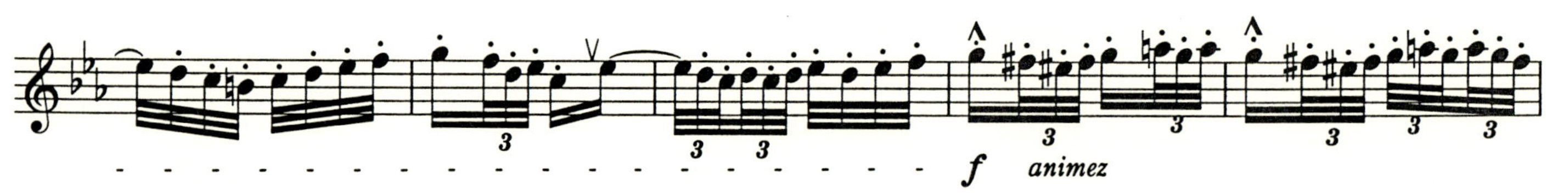

léger cédez
subito pp
animez
rit.
a tempo
cresc. - - - - - élargir
f
rit.
a tempo
ff
cédez
rit.
a tempo
rit.
a tempo
pp
pp
poco a
poco accelerando
pp
(♪=116)
cresc. - - - - animez
ff